Cute As a Bug's Ear
Copyright © 2018 by Olivia Worthen

All rights reserved. No part of this publication may be reproduced, distributed, or transmitted in any form or by any means, including photocopying, recording, or other electronic or mechanical methods, without the prior written permission of the publisher or author, except in the case of brief quotations embodied in critical reviews and certain other noncommercial uses permitted by copyright law. For permission requests, contact the publisher through the website below.

Day Agency
South Jordan, UT 84009
www.dayagency.com

Cover Design and Interior layout: Dayna Linton, Day Agency

Library of Congress: Pending

ISBN: 978-0-9996833-1-6

First Edition
10 9 8 7 6 5 4 3 2 1
Printed in the United States of America

Cute As A Bug's Ear

by Olivia Worthen

Illustrated by

Katherine Hamilton Koy

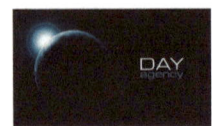

Cute as A Bug's Ear

Dedicated to my many cousins, aunts, uncles and grandparents who have always offered never ending love and support throughout the years.

Melanie and Olivia were cousins who lived in a small country town right across the street from one another. They enjoyed spending as much time together as possible. Their grandma would often tell them she thought they were as close as two peas in a pod because she rarely saw one without the other.

These two cousins had become, as far as they were concerned, expert hut builders. Just recently they made the most fantastic hut between the two apple trees that grew in Olivia's backyard.

The imagination of these two little girls seemed to be the fuel for not only hut building, but many other adventure-filled days.

On one such day, Melanie appeared at Olivia's house in her beautiful white princess dress. Upon seeing Melanie in this particular dress, Olivia knew it was to be "Princess Day," and so she quickly slipped into her green princess dress. She said goodbye to her mom, and the girls were off to Melanie's house.

They both realized before "Princess Day" could really begin; they needed to make their crowns. After all, a princess must have a crown.

The cousins always made their crowns by braiding the stems of clover blossoms.

Melanie had a big backyard, and that's where the clover grew. There were patches scattered throughout the grass which could easily be seen because of the little white blossoms popping up here and there throughout the lawn.

The girls discovered that the long-stemmed clovers needed to braid crowns grew along the back fence.

So, it was by the fence that they carefully selected a handful of the clovers and then sat down on the garden bench to start braiding. It was a lot of work and not quite as simple as braiding their own hair or the hair of their dolls.

With the crowns finally finished, they carefully placed them on top of their heads.

"I'm Princess Clover Blossom," said Olivia with a royal curtsy.

"And, I'll be Princess Buttercup," exclaimed Melanie.

Just at that moment, they happened to look across the white picket fence and noticed their grandma in her backyard hanging clothes on the clothesline to dry in the warm sunlight.

"Let's go show Grandma our crowns," suggested Olivia.

The girls held hands and skipped next door to their grandma's house.

"Grandma, it's us, Princess Clover Blossom and Princess Buttercup," said Melanie.

The girls twirled around in their princess dresses to show their grandma just how beautiful they felt.

Their grandma looked lovingly at her granddaughters in their pretty little dresses. She tenderly touched the clover crowns on their heads.

"Oh, my heavens," she said. "You girls are just as cute as a bug's ear." The girls giggled. They had never actually seen a bug's ear and wondered for a moment if bugs really *did* have cute ears. Then they waved goodbye to their grandma and skipped back over to Melanie's yard into the land of make-believe where wishes could be granted, and dreams could come true among the fragrant clover blossoms.

As they played, they didn't notice a bumblebee busily buzzing among the clover blossoms.

Suddenly, in the middle of a twirl, Olivia felt a sting on her leg. She instantly knew what had happened. She'd been stung by a bumblebee!

Tears came to her eyes, and she started to cry. Melanie quickly ran over and saw the red mark on Olivia's leg. She put her arm around her cousin's shoulder and gently guided her over to the garden bench.

"Wait here," she said, I'll get some ice to put on the sting." Moments later Melanie returned with the ice wrapped in a napkin. Olivia held the ice on the sting while her cousin sat next to her until she started feeling better.

"Do you think that bumblebees really have cute ears?" wondered Olivia. She wasn't thinking nice thoughts about the bee that had just stung her leg.

"I don't know," replied Melanie thoughtfully. Both girls remained silent for a moment or two lost in their thoughts.

It wasn't very long until the two princesses were twirling and dancing again in their make-believe princess world. A magical kingdom of their own right in Melanie's backyard.

"Tomorrow," said Melanie, right in the middle of a twirl, "We should play with paper dolls."

"Yes, we should," said Olivia, as she looked into the sky with visions of paper dolls already forming in her imagination.

It was always so much fun to play with her cousin who had such wonderful ideas and just happened to be her very best friend as well.

How to Braid a Princess Crown

1. Gather a bunch of clover blossoms with long stems.

2. Select 3 blossoms and start braiding the stems.

3. Tie the end of the stems with a thin ribbon or string.

4. Place three more blossoms on top of the tie. Tie them on and start braiding the new stems.

5. Continue adding new blossoms until long enough for a crown.

6. Tie the end of the string of blossoms to the beginning.

About the Author

Olivia Worthen was an Elementary School Teacher and Reading Specialist for 37 years and has always enjoyed writing short stories and poetry. She especially loved incorporating Writer's Workshop into her daily curriculum, teaching her students to find their voice through writing.

She and her husband, David, are the parents of six children and 18 grandchildren. They live in South Jordan, Utah.

www.ingramcontent.com/pod-product-compliance
Lightning Source LLC
Chambersburg PA
CBHW040738150426
42811CB00064B/1782